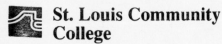

How to Prepare and Present

Roughs, Comps, and Mock-ups

How to Prepare and Present

Roughs, Comps, and Mock-ups

ART DIRECTION BOOK COMPANY
NEW YORK

Library of Congress Catalog Card Number: 84-071518
ISBN: 0-88108-014-4

Printed in the United States of America

Published by
ART DIRECTION BOOK COMPANY
10 East 39th Street
New York, New York 10016

Acknowledgement

I would like to thank Jack Anderson of John Hornell Design Works in Seattle, Washington for loaning so many examples of his work for inclusion in this book. His generosity is greatly appreciated. I would also like to thank Lauren Bernstein for her editorial assistance.

Contents

I
Introduction

The Role of Presentation in the Design Process

Presentation is a vital and complex part of the design process. For most designers, the presentation is the point of sale; it is the client presentation that affords you the opportunity to explain your ideas and design solutions.

Successful designers understand that the more descriptive their presentation materials are, the more likely their ideas will be understood and accepted by the client. The better presentations, though, are not necessarily elaborate. Effective presentations can range from loose sketches to extraordinarily detailed mock-ups. An effective presentation is one that shows and tells a client what he or she needs to know about your ideas. Each designer eventually develops a comfortable vocabulary of presentation techniques he or she can use with success.

This book offers samples of many of the styles and techniques designers use to communicate visual ideas to clients. The purpose of this book is to help the designer select the style and comping technique appropriate to each job so that the designer's ideas are presented properly.

Clients don't like surprises

The ideal designer/client relationship is long term, profitable for both parties, interesting, challenging, and is based on mutual respect. There is little room for unpleasant surprises in the design process. Comps, roughs, and mock-ups help to eliminate uncertainties for your client, preventing professional and even legal problems for you later on.

Although this book concentrates on the presentation stage of a project, comps, roughs, and mock-ups are important to you while you are in the process of designing a piece, long before your presentation to the client. Few designers have the capacity to accurately visualize a piece in their minds without seeing it in some physical form. Design pieces are composed of obvious and subtle details, and relying on your imagination to work out those elements is tricky business. As the best designers know, there is no shame in relying on comps and roughs to pre-visualize design ideas.

Definition of Terms

For this book, these terms will be used as follows: *Rough:* A sketch. A loose rendering or generalized model, showing the basic elements in a design or design product. *Comp (comprehensive):* A detailed representation of a design or design product. Type, illustrations, photographs, paper stock, and layout are rendered closely enough to the finished product to convey an accurate impression of the printed or constructed piece. *Mock-up:* A facsimile of a printed or constructed design product. A three-dimensional model or assembled, one-of-a-kind representation.

Selecting an appropriate presentation style

Each designer develops a presentation vocabulary to accommodate the needs and expectations of each client. A new design assignment from a new client often requires a fully detailed comp. An established client more familiar with your work might only need to see a developed rough. The selection of the appropriate presentation method depends upon a knowledge of your client's expectations, the requirements of the project, and an intuitive understanding of what it will take to communicate your ideas to your client. You also need a clear idea of what you, your staff support, or your suppliers (production assistant, typesetter, photographer, printer, etc.) will need to produce the piece once it has been approved for production.

Opinions on the proper amount of detail for a comp vary with each designer. One well-known graphic designer does not show a client a comp until all of the copy has been typeset and a full color comp prepared. Another equally well-known designer insists that design options occur to her up to the moment of printing the piece, and that by preparing a comp that is too tight, she is denying herself the possibility of changing the piece along the way. Interestingly, both approaches are hard-nosed. The first designer assumes that the client will absorb the extra production expenses to produce a secure comp. The second assumes that artistic freedom can keep a design in limbo until the piece is actually printed. Most designers are not as fortunate or (hard-nosed) as these two, and have to learn to be accommodating to the client without sacrificing crucial design control. A designer needs to learn what works for himself, and for each client.

It takes time and money to prepare a tight comp, but if that is what it takes for you or your client to visualize the finished product, then a tight comp is a necessity. If a rough is enough for you and your client to work from, then that is an appropriate style.

In any case, the presentation process is so central to the design process, no designer can afford to ignore the importance of a well-considered and well-prepared rough, comp, or mock-up for each design project.

Quality and Craft

Quality and craft are universally admired and respected, and in the preparation of presentation materials this is especially true. As a designer you should establish a level of quality for your firm and the work it produces, and then work to maintain that level of quality in your presentation materials and in the finished products.

Since the preparation of presentations is frequently done under severe deadline pressures, you need to select your presentation methods with an eye for practicality, effectiveness and uniformity. It would be unfortunate to run out of time before all of your materials were complete, or to have half of your presentation done very nicely, and the other half obviously thrown together in a panic. Better that all of your presentation is completed to the same degree of finish.

Attention to the details that indicate quality take time, practice, and perseverance to maintain. Still, it is never difficult to defend the importance of quality to your client, if what you are showing them is of quality itself.

II
Type Indication and Comping Techniques

Type Indication

Since text and display type are central to so many graphic design projects, it is important for designers to understand the various ways display and text type can be represented on a rough or comp.

The issue is simple; you want an accurate impression of how the type relates to the total design project. That includes how much type fits on each page, the proportion of the type to the illustrations, how much white space there will be, what type sizes are to be used, and how type on facing pages will relate. Since text type is usually the heart of a publication, we will begin with the ways to indicate text type.

Text Type

When a designer lays out a page with text on it, many design decisions are considered, evaluated, and dismissed before one is selected. Does the design call for justified columns, flush right or flush left arrangement? How much leading should be allowed? How long should the line measure be? How much indentation is acceptable? How much space between columns? How many columns per page? These are all important decisions.

Since text type characters are usually small in relation to the other elements on a page—like white space, illustrations, photographs, or headlines—most designers choose to give an impression of the type rather than a typeset rendering of the text. The letter forms in comps of this detail are less important than the effect of their weight in line form. Therefore, an indication of type size and weight on the page is a basic first step.

There are several methods to indicate text type. The important elements to consider are: which method conveys the weight of the type best, which looks cleaner on the comp, and which method takes the least amount of time to draw properly?

Pencil Line, Ink Line, and Greeking

Pencil line indication is the traditional method. It is simple, direct, flexible and, if properly rendered, can duplicate the weight and general impression of typesetting. With practice and skill, pencil indication is extremely effective.

Ink line indication is similar to pencil line indication, except that it looks definite, and is more permanent and less likely to smudge than pencil indication.

Greeking is text type made from random words (often gibberish) of the approximate size, style, and weight of the printed piece. It is sold as transfer rub-down, and adhesive plastic film. Some designers make paper Greeking by photocopying type samples of the text type they want to use, and then cutting, gluing, and positioning the type onto a dummy layout to get a more accurate impression of the finished piece.

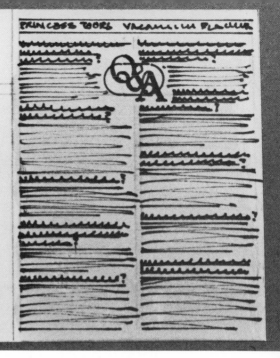

From the earliest stages of a design project the client and the designer need to feel comfortable with the material that will eventually be included in the final design. Roughs help both parties visualize the basic relationships and general design approach without allowing them to become trapped in matters of secondary detail. In this rough, the designer is thinking on paper with small, rough sketches of each spread. For books or catalogues, these sketches can be very small, laid out in sequence on a piece of matteboard to show the client the entire project at a glance. This sample is about the size of a business card.

These two roughs clearly show placement and scale of type and the other essential design elements in reduced scale.

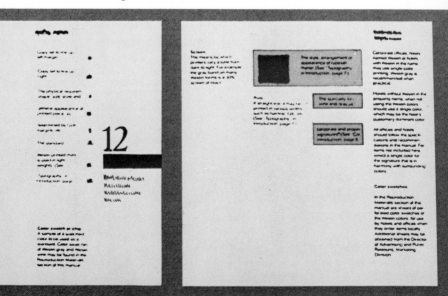

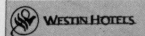

Group Insurance Enrollment and Change Card

A. Employee Data

Name _____ Social Security No. _____
           Last   First   Initial

Birthdate _____ Within Hire Date: _____ Sex _____ Citizenship _____

B. Comprehensive Health Care:

Dependent(s): (For Future Changes)   Acquired   Terminated

I wish the following dependent(s) covered:

Name	Relationship	Date of Birth	Effective Date

Employee Effective Date: _____ Hotel _____

Employee & above dependent(s) will be covered under the following plans:

Connecticut General: ☐ Medical ☐ Dental   HMO: ☐ Medical ☐ Dental

It would be hard for a designer to get much more definite about the way this card will look once printed. Forms are complex design problems with many important elements. This designer understands how much production time he is saving later on by being this specific at the comp stage. A typesetter would have little problem duplicating this form on the keyboard in one pass.

8

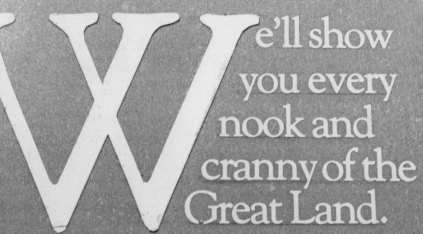

We'll show you every nook and cranny of the Great Land.

Thus, th
ledge in th
the invent
tic machir
discovery,
the physic
space by r
signal, an
nas been
Large are
recently
in mathe
and in do
tentlv up
the gene

ry of the E.glish Language nas been prepared. It is an entirely new dictionary, written in midcentury ror twentieth-c ntury users. socie cause it is fully up to date and thoroughly

The large "W" was cut from white paper and glued to the comp to show the effect of white on colored background. The other white type is custom-made rubdown transfer type. The black text type is rubdown Greeking.

Land is a Basis of Wealth

There are many reasons why land has always attracted the sophisticated investor. The earth is one of the most basic of all natural resources and is one of the few commodities man cannot reproduce. Since the beginning of civilization, land has been a major source of wealth. As such, it continues to be one of man's most highly valued treasures.

Wealth cannot be accumulated by savings retained from salaries and wages, despite the fact that during a lifetime the average person both earns and spends a small fortune. Such earnings must be invested wisely if they are to grow in the face of unparalleled increases in the cost of living and decreases in the purchasing power of paper currencies.

Historically, as other tangible assets fluctuate in worth, land either holds its value in times of recession or enjoys a high rate of appreciation during prosperous times when development is occurring in major growth areas, thus providing an excellent hedge against inflation.

Unlike many investment mediums, the tax aspects of land investment are straightforward and predictable. Land investments, as typically sponsored by The Myers Group, enjoy substantial tax deductions during the holding period. The profit realized at the time of sale is taxed at the lower long-term capital gain rates.

The goal of land investment is to assure the investor the safest, largest, and most consistent return, while at the same time applying the principal of leverage to minimize the investor's capital outlay. Land should be viewed as a basic and essential element in any well-conceived investment portfolio, providing balance to other types of investments.

Meeting these objectives requires professional experience, analysis, and forecasting—services provided by the staff of The Myers Group.

These two figures show the comp and the final printed piece. Notice the difference in text type styles and subhead indication. The photographs are suggested with simple gestural lines drawn

THE MYERS GROUP

A Conservative Approach for the Cautious Investor

The Myers Group is one of the largest sponsors of privately offered land investment limited partnerships in the United States in terms of properties acquired and dollar amount raised and/or committed.

Through the offering of limited partnership interests, The Myers Group provides the opportunity for sophisticated investors to participate in the ownership of prime, strategically-located land parcels, normally available only to very wealthy individuals or large institutions.

An investment in a limited partnership interest allows the investor to benefit from group investment in professionally selected and managed land.

Limited partnerships sponsored by The Myers Group provide a hedge against both inflation and taxation...offering a means by which investors can more effectively cope with the uncertainties of today's economy.

The Myers Group has designed limited partnerships to give the individual investor the opportunity to balance his portfolio by taking a limited risk position in one of the most historically sought-after and conservative classes of real estate—well-located prime investment land.

A Conservative Approach for the Cautious Investor

on tissue paper. Color is applied on the back of the tissue with felt tip pen. The tissue was then spray-glued and mounted onto a paper comparable in weight to the finished piece.

The quality of any of these methods is determined by how closely the text type resembles the finished printed piece, and how carefully it is applied.

Headlines, Subheads, and Display Type

Headlines, subheads, and display type are basic to most graphic design projects. Knowing how to indicate them is an elementary skill. Although the text may contain the important information in a publication or ad, the heads and subheads give the piece its initial appeal, character, and sense of design and style. Since display type is larger than text type, and since line length and character size can be critical elements in a comp, the designer must indicate them with care. For text type, a series of drawn parallel lines are adequate—but headline characters need to be rendered.

Characteristics of a typeface become more apparent in larger form: the serif details, width of the strokes, length of ascenders and descenders, capitalization style, letter height, and letter and word spacing. The larger the letters, the more accurately your letter forms should be drawn.

For most designers working today, drawing type freehand is difficult, time consuming, and frequently inaccurate. It is a handy skill to have, and an enviable one, but for all of the designers who never had the advantage of an extensive and traditional typography or calligraphy education, there are lots of alternatives to freehand drawing of type—all of them at least as satisfying and functional as the traditional approach. These include:

1. Tracing directly from a type sample.
2. Enlarging or reducing a type sample, and then tracing or drawing.
3. Transfer type enlarged or reduced, and then tracing or drawing.
4. Transfer type applied directly onto the comp.

We will discuss each method in turn, but since several of the techniques may involve changing the size of the type from its original size, we will first discuss the ways to enlarge and reduce type. These methods also apply to line art.

Reverse type on colored background can be indicated in several ways. Here, white tempera paint, thinned with water, was applied with a ruling pen. Tempera is delicate on some surfaces. Spraying with fixative is usually a good idea with this method.

Metallic type can be indicated by using a puddle of ink from a metallic felt marker, applied with a brush.

Getting complex typography to wrap around forms can be difficult. Here, custom rubdown transfer type was applied, one word
at a time, to an acetate overlay. Once the placement of the type is
established, the typographer will have a far easier job setting the
final type into exact position. This is a good example of how a
tight comp can be especially helpful to the production artists and
suppliers.

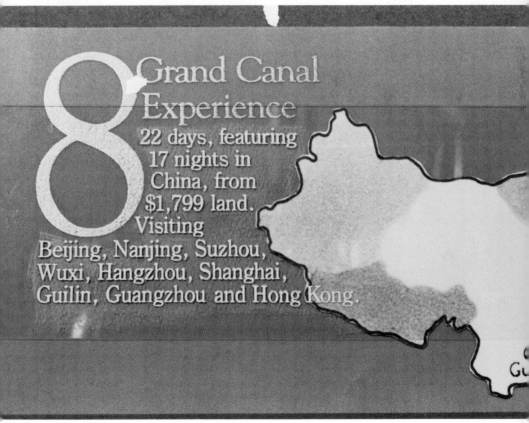

8 Grand Canal
Experience
22 days, featuring
17 nights in
China, from
$1,799 land.
Visiting
Beijing, Nanjing, Suzhou,
Wuxi, Hangzhou, Shanghai,
Guilin, Guangzhou and Hong Kong.

PRINCESS TOURS VACATION PLANNER

From Fairbanks

BAKE An authentic Alaskan meal you'll remember for
esh from Sitka. Halibut from the icy waters of
Ribs barbecued over alderwood to give them that special
-you-can-eat salad bar, sourdough
blueberry cake and beverage
ilable). Served nightly, 5 p.m.
; transfer to and from your hotel.

Adults $ _____
Children under 12 $ _____

1 DAY Jet to the "top of the
ow, northermost point of the
ontinent. See a sun that never
r days. The multi-million dollar
nds its way down from the
n how the Eskimo maintains life
Arctic environment. See an Eskimo blanket toss and
; hear a fascinating description of the Eskimo whale
airbanks by jet.

	Tour Price	Tax	Estimated Air Cost
. . . .$	_____	_____	_____
. . . .$	_____	_____	_____

:COVERY Be on board as the sternwheeler *Discovery*
makes its daily cruise down the
Chena and Tanana Rivers. Along the
30-mile excursion, see a home
steader's cabin. A bush airstrip. An

OPTIONAL TOURS

ANCHORAGE FROM THE AIR Few cities command such i
from the air. In every direction you'll see mountain rang
rugged mountains etched by meandering streams and l.
mitting, you can clearly see Mt. McKinley standing hig
magnificent sight. Transfers between hotel and airfield
utes in the air.

CROW CREEK GOLD MINING Relive th
area experienced over 80 years ago-
for gold! Travel by van or motor coacl
oldest gold mining district in Alaska.
just like it did back in 1898.) Pan for
coffee/donut break in the old mining
Return to your hotel. Approximately

EAGLE RIVER NATURE TRAIL Meet yc
of the hotel at 7 p.m. for a van ride t
area, part of the Chugach State Park. Along the 2½ hor
guide will identify the flora and fauna, explain the geo
and describe the park's natural history. Pause along the
Chugach Mountains for a view of Turnagain and Knik A
Ocean and of the Anchorage "Bowl." Return to hotel.

KOTZEBUE, 1 DAY Jet across the Arctic Circle to the lar
sun, and Kotzebue, second largest
Eskimo village in Alaska. Walk along
"main street" on the beach and see
drying racks loaded with salmon and
whale meat. Visit a fish camp, a gen-

This detail of a mock-up shows the actual type in place, with
photographs, headlines, rules, and decorative elements. The
photocopy is on colored paper, though. The designer photocopied the comp onto Pantone paper, probably in duplicate, so
that his client could pass it around to the decision makers and
detail checkers in the company for their final approval.

Carnegie**International**
Seattle Art Museum · Volunteer Park
February 10 – March 27, 1983

ergat. Nos amice et nebevol molestias access potest fier
pecun modut est neque nonor imper ned libiding gen epular religuard
magist and dedocendesse videantur. Invitat igitur vera ratio bene sanos ad au
efficerd possit duo conetud notiner si effecerit, et opos vel fortunag vel

praesent iupratem
est laborum et dolor fuga
id quod maxim placeat facer
atib saepe eveniet

est ao quiet.

Posters can be comped to scale, rather than full-size. This one is 50% of the final printed piece. The main lines of type were set and the smaller copy below is actually Greeking. The artwork is an R print.

Changing the Size of Your Type Sample

In the last few years, the number of different ways to enlarge or reduce type and line art has increased. You can photostat the type. Some copying machines have reducing and enlarging capabilities, and there are several projection devices in common use in design studios.

Here is the same type enlarged by photostat in several sizes.

Photostats

Photostats can be made to any size. The copies can be extremely clean, and are available in positive or negative (reverse) form on paper and film. The principal disadvantage of this method is that it costs more than the other processes; even a small photostat costs several dollars. Unless you have direct access to a stat camera, it can take longer than the other methods. Sources for photostats can be found in the Yellow Pages listed under Photocopying.

A very light photocopy of type can be colored with pencil or felt marker.

This logotype was photocopied onto colored paper. Since it will finally appear in the piece as reverse type on colored background, white tempera brushed on was a good way to indicate that kind of treatment.

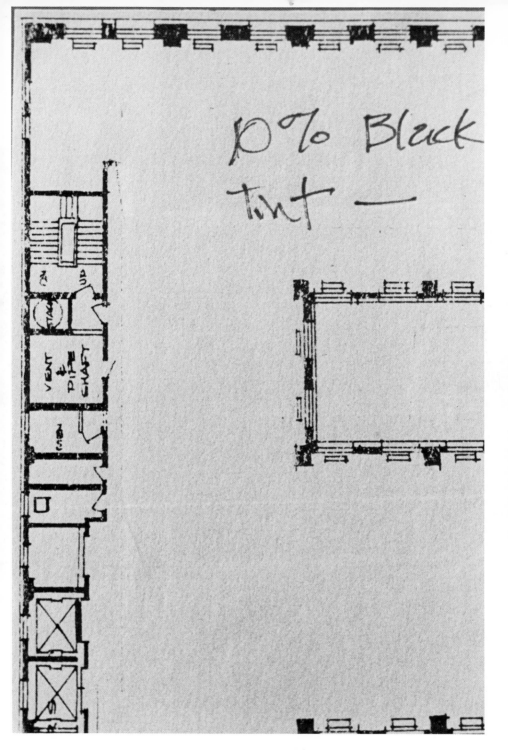

This floorplan was photocopied onto uncoated colored paper and spray glued to the comp. Photocopy machines can be amazingly versatile tools for preparing comps.

Copier Machines

Xerographic copiers have become amazingy versatile design tools. While most copiers only produce same size copies of originals, some machines offer a choice of reduction sizes. Some more elaborate machines have thorough reducing and enlarging capabilities, and can print on larger paper than regular copiers. These copies are not as clean as photostats, but they are substantially less expensive, and for most comping purposes they are perfectly adequate.

You may have to spend some time finding a conveniently located copier with variable enlarging or reducing capabilities. They are usually found in high volume copying companies like blueprint houses that service architectural or engineering firms. The Yellow Pages lists them under Blue printers or Photocopying.

The copiers with only two or three reduction sizes can be helpful, too, if you can learn how to use the sizes or combination of sizes. For example, you can reduce an original type sample, and then reduce that copy one step again or if you have a type sample in 48 point and you want to reduce it to 36 point, you can reduce it 77% with the copier and approximate 36 point type. Reduce that copy by 77% and you will have an example of 28 point type. Ultimately, however, the variable size copier is much more versatile.

Copy machines cannot make reverses out of positive originals the way a photostat process can, but many copier machines can copy onto sheets of acetate or polyester film, which might be heplful in some applications, *i.e.*, for tracing type on a light table.

Projection techniques

For most design studios, opaque projection is the most affordable method for enlarging and reducing type and line art for comps. It requires an initial investment for the projector, and from then on, the operating expenses are minimal. There are two styles of opaque projectors, although they both work on a similar principle, and there is also a device which is an optical tool that can work like a very simple projector.

The Artograph style projector uses flat art as original material. The image is projected through a lens. The projector is raised or lowered to increase or reduce the size of the image. The quality of the image depends upon the quality of the lens, the distance the image is projected, and the darkness of the room. The advantages of this style of projector are that you can project onto a work table for normal enlargements and reductions, or you can swing the unit around so that it projects onto the floor for much greater enlargement. The projector has the capability for backlighting to project slides and transparencies. The main advantage, though, is that you can project onto a piece of opaque paper or any other kind of drawing surface. The disadvantages are that your original must be smaller than a square foot, or it has to be foldable down to less than a square foot to fit into the machine's copyboard, and you need a relatively dark room.

The Lucygraph style projector's main advantage is that you can fit a larger original into the copyboard, but since the image is projected up onto a piece of glass from below, your enlargement capability is limited. You are further restricted by the surface area from which you can trace. Also, since the image is projected from below onto clear glass, you have to trace the image onto frosted film or tracing paper; you can't trace or draw the image directly onto an opaque surface. Most Lucygraphs do not have light boxes built into their copyboards, so it is difficult to project slides or transparencies for tracing. Still, designers have relied on this style of projector for years, with satisfying results.

Camera Lucida

The least expensive, and for some applications, the most versatile is the Camera Lucida. A small, optical tool with a prism and a set of lenses, this device lets you draw from life, from type samples, and from any kind of artwork, onto any surface, opaque or not. It does not allow you to draw directly from slides or transparencies. It is also somewhat awkward to use.

With the enlarging and reducing techniques explained, we can go onto the four ways to indicate headlines, subheads, and display type.

1. Tracing directly from a type sample If you have a type sample book with a complete alphabet in the size and style you need for your comp, you are in luck. With tracing paper, a pencil, pen, or felt pen, you can trace the display type to the degree of finish that the comp requires. You should end up with a good approximation of how the type will look.

2. Enlarging or reducing the type sample, and then tracing or drawing If you have a complete alphabet in the right style but the wrong size, you can use one of the several enlargement or reduction methods previously discussed. If your alphabet is 36 point type and you need a 72 point headline, you can have a photostat copy made at 200%, a copy machine enlargement at 200%, or you could put the alphabet into a projector and draw or trace the type to the correct size.

3. Transfer type enlarged or reduced, and then tracing or drawing Transfer type to spell words in headline, and then enlarge or reduce if necessary, and then trace.

4. Transfer type applied directly onto the comp If you have the correct size transfer lettering, you can just apply it directly. As a rule, comps look better if the headline style is consistent; if you use transfer type for one headline, you should use it for all of the headlines. If you don't have enough transfer type for the entire comp, then stick to a drawn or traced style.

3-M makes a tape that is less sticky than normal transparent tape. Here, rubdown type is applied to the tape. It can be lifted and repositioned on the rough or comp to show the designer how it will eventually look. It is unnecessary to go to the trouble of drawing the type many times in different positions.

5. Transfer or trace type on low-stick tape   A recent product on the market is low stick frosted tape, which allows you to reposition the tape without damaging the paper surface of the comp. This technique is especially helpful if you are not sure exactly where you want to place the type. Cut a length of tape from the roll. Transfer òr trace the type onto the tape, and position it onto the comp. When properly positioned, trim excess tape off with an x-acto knife.

This spread is from a Letraset catalogue. It shows the complete alphabet in four typefaces, as well as the variety of sizes in which each alphabet is available.

Transfer lettering

Transfer lettering, also known as rubdown lettering, has become enormously popular. For the trained designer, it is a wonderful aid that allows and encourages experimentation and tighter roughs, comps and mock-ups.

The following examples describe several of the ways rubdown type can be used in the comp stage of a design project. Color rubdown type and other color techniques will be discussed in Chapter V.

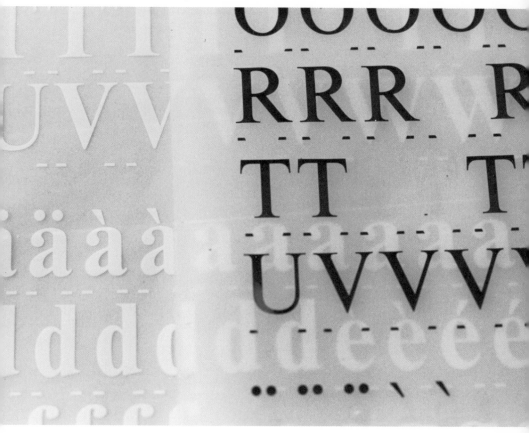

Rubdown transfer type is commonly available in white and black. Other colors of some faces are also available.

These burnishers are used to transfer type.

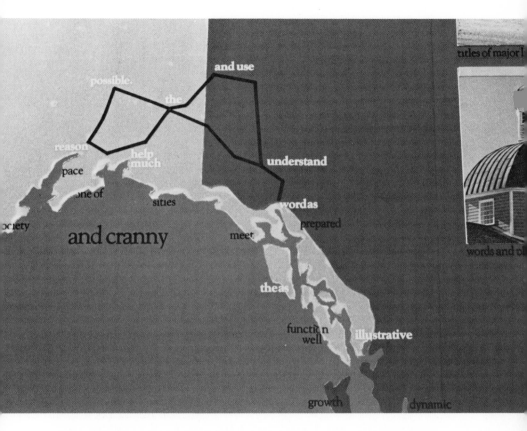

This detail of a map (also shown on page 37) shows the application of black and white rubdown transfer type on colored backgrounds. Given the surface of color overlay film it would be difficult to properly indicate type any other way.

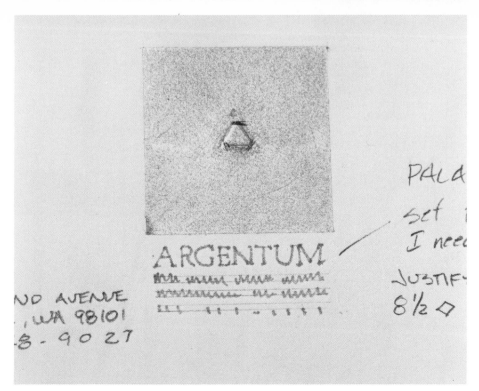

Embossing can also be indicated by cutting out a matchboard die and very carefully rubbing the paper from the back with a burnisher, molding the paper to the shape of the die.

Die cutting can be comped by carefully cutting out the design with an exacto knife.

This comp for a letterhead uses a couple of techniques. The white letters are cut out with an x-acto knife. The other parts of the design are indicated in several colors of felt pen ink. White is the most difficult value to indicate on colored paper. White ink is usually too thin to cover properly, and although white tempera thinned and applied with a ruling pen can work, for smaller applications, cutout paper or white rubdown transfer type is usually the most successful technique.

III
Comps for Illustrations

Illustrations and photographs are the focus of so many graphic and advertising projects, yet they can be difficult for clients to visualize in rough and comp stages of a project. These next two chapters will discuss the important points of illustration and photography roughs and comps.

This series of photographs shows the progression of an illustration from its earliest stages through to final printed result. On the rough, the instructions to the illustrator are clearly indicated. In the comp, all of the refinements to the design are indicated on the sheet of paper. The final figure shows the printed piece.

Working with Illustration in a Design Project

As the designer, if you decide that an illustration (not your own) is an appropriate approach to the problem, you face several issues. You need to explain to the client why illustration is required, how elaborate that illustration needs to be, and what information it needs to convey. Secondly, you need to give the client some idea of what the illustration will look like, and how it will fit into the entire design. Finally, you need to explain to the illustrator what you and your client expect and require.

Let's assume that you have managed the first step, and the client has agreed to illustration and subject matter. The next step is to work up a sketch. In that sketch you make some decisions about composition and style. Will it be a painting? Will it be pen and ink, wash, or pencil illustration? Will it be printed in one, two, three, or four colors? Tightly rendered, naturalistic, impressionistic, highly stylized, strongly graphic, traditional or entirely abstract?

Your sketch should convey the impression of the illustration, if not all the details and subtleties. Indicate the size and location of the illustration to get a feeling for the subject, page balance, color and scale relationships for your own satisfaction. Some designers can devise a satisfactory rough with a few gesture lines; others prefer more detailed drawings.

Any rough drawing you show to a client, though, should be prepared for his mind's eye, not yours. It should contain indication of details that are most important to him, be they subject or stylistic points.

If you have a particular illustrator in mind for the project, get examples of his work to take along to the presentation, to give the client a better idea of the illustrator's style. If you haven't decided upon an illustrator, but you know what style you are after, bring style samples.

If the subject matter is technical or highly detailed, gather scrap photos or drawings of the items to be included in the illustration for the client to verify and approve. Changing an illustration after it is drawn because of improper preparation at the beginning is especially aggravating for illustrators. Stylistic decisions about charts, maps, and technical illustrations should be made early on as well. There is extraordinary variety in illustration, and since design solutions have become so diverse, it makes sense to determine the look of the illustrations as the design solution begins to evolve.

A map, prepared with felt marker, technical pens and white paint on tissue paper, helped give the client a clear idea of how the project would look in its final printed form.

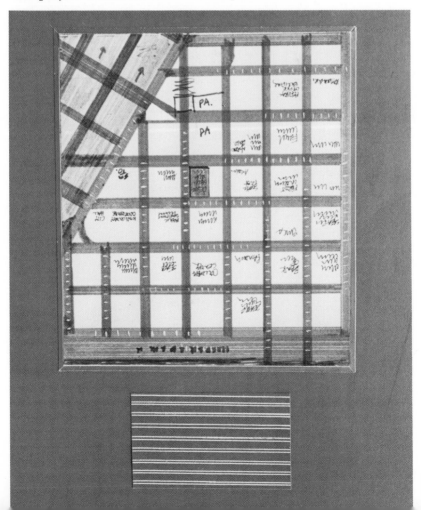

A designer who is his own illustrator is in a convenient position, since his sketches will eventually become the finished illustration. He doesn't need to go through another step or two of communication with a third party. He also has the advantage of speaking to the client directly, and designing the illustration and layout simultaneously.

This rough isn't any larger, but it is more refined. Some designers find this method of presentation particularly effective. They are tight enough for the client to visualize the design, but general enough to prevent the client from getting distracted by the type size, line breaks or word and photo selection.

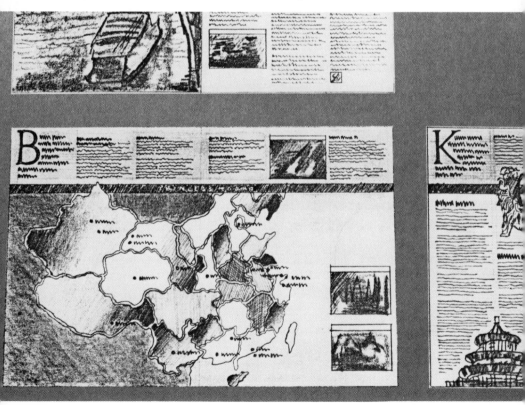

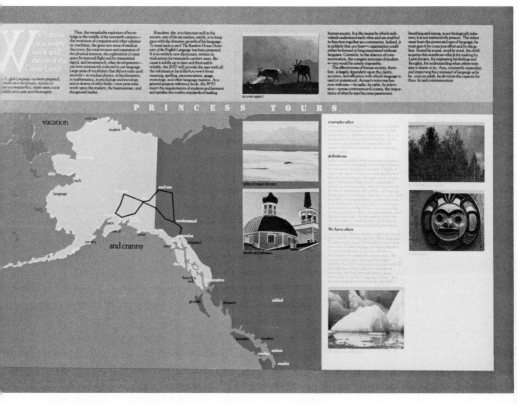

This comp is for the same project, but at a later stage. It has been prepared to its final 8½" × 11" size, with color overlay film, border tape, rubdown transfer type, photographs either furnished by the client or pulled from other magazines. At this stage of the design, the client has already agreed to the design approach and can now begin to make final content decisions. Since there are so many different kinds of graphic materials used on this comp, it was a good idea to mount it on matteboard so that parts of the illustration won't pop off as easily.

Working Drawings for the Illustrator

If you hire an illustrator for an assignment, find out how he or she prefers to work with the client; some like to discuss the project directly with the client, others only work with art director. Some clients will want you to handle all of the details.

Meet with the illustrator to determine what he needs from you in art direction, scrap, or technical details. Show him the sketch you prepared for the client. Gather his suggestions, explain which details are essential, and which stylistic decisions you and your client expect.

From this point the illustrator can prepare a tighter rough for you and your client to approve or correct before making the final artwork. Most of the problems that illustrators get into with a client occur when important information isn't explained properly by the client or art director, and the most frustrating part about these kinds of communication problems is that they are so easy to avoid.

At the stage where a rough is presented there is the possibility that the client will disapprove of the illustration altogether. Find out from the client if the problems are minor and easily repaired. If the client is passionate in his rejection, it may be wise to pay the illustrator for his work to that point, and then go looking for another illustrator. Better that you resolve a difficult problem at an early stage than try to force the client to accept something he doesn't want or like. A more common problem, though, is that a client can't decide if he likes the illustration. This is where your opinion can be valuable. If you have his trust you can make a strong case for the illustration, if indeed, you think it is appropriate to the design problem. If you don't like the illustration either, you can give it your honest appraisal. Do not let yourself get into a position of defending inferior or inappropriate work to a client; it only reflects badly on your professionalism.

Working with Finished Illustrations

Once an illustration has been approved for a design project, you may want to photocopy it to the finished size so that you can see how it will look in its final printed form. There are several methods to use.

A photostat here served two functions. One was to show the client the scale of the photograph. The second was to show the printer the exact positioning of the image. The photostat was reduced to the same percentage reduction as the final halftone.

Photostat: If the illustration is a line drawing with strong blacks and whites, a simple xerographic copy or a photostat will work well. If the illustration needs to be sized, a variable size copier could be used.

If the illustration has grey values that will drop out in a line shot, you might want to get a half-tone photostat. The process is similar to a line stat except that a half-tone screen is used to help retain the grey tones in the illustration. This extra step costs a little more than a line shot. You may be asked which line screen you want used. Halftone screens come in a variety of dot sizes, from very coarse (65 line) to very fine (150 line). If this screen stat is used only to allow you to see how the illustration will look in its final size, then select a screen that will approximate the final printed piece. For example if you are preparing a newspaper ad, the illustration will probably be printed in 65 to 85 line screen. If it's a magazine ad on finer paper, a 133 line screen is more common. If you are preparing a finely printed annual report, you should use a 150 line screen.

Color illustrations present other problems, but there are ways to enlarge, reduce, or reproduce to size for comps and mock-ups.

Color Stats: A relatively new method of a single copy color reproduction is the color photostat. The process is similar to black-and-white stat work; the sizing and processing and speed are shared features. It isn't as widely available as black-and-white stat work, but it is less expensive and much faster than the next technique.

Color Photos: The traditional way to reproduce a color photograph to size is to enlarge the original negative and print the size you want it for your mock-up or comp. This technique involves some time and expense. Custom photo labs can assist you with this technique. You should be prepared to tell the lab exactly how large you want the finished photo print to turn out.

If the illustration is the same size as the finished, printed reproduction, you have one more way to reproduce a copy for a mock-up or comp—color xerox. Since direct color reproduction is one to one, you can't enlarge or reduce the image to fit, unless you use slide enlargement. Color rendition and quality are not accurate either, and might not give you an acceptable rendition of the illustration. Speed is this method's chief advantage, and with a skillful operator color xerox can be an effective comping technique.

IV
Roughs for Photographs

Since photography is based in reality, with real models, props, locations, and effects, an art director and designer face a set of problems different than the ones discussed in the previous chapter on working with illustration.

For the art director, there are several ways to use photography in a design project. He can use photographs that already exist; the client can supply photographs from which to choose; the designer can select from the files of stock photo agencies; the designer can also hire a photographer to take new photographs. Since this last option usually requires roughs at an earlier stage in the design process, we will discuss it first.

Say that you are a designer with a catalogue to produce. You know the products you want to include in the layout and how large they will be. You will want to show the photographer how his photos will be used to give him

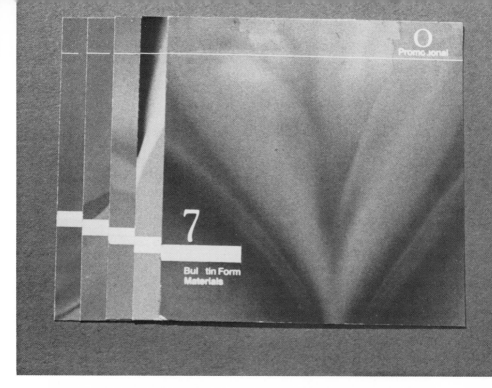

These comps are a fraction of their final printed size. Each of the pages are a few inches square. At a glance they give the client an overview of how the entire package of printed material will function. They show scale of type, relationships of the photographs, charts and type. Presenting a project like this in miniature can be extremely effective. Designs with strong grids become very clear and striking when they are reduced. These pages were mounted onto one large presentation board.

an idea of your concept and art direction for the assignment. Your roughs should include some basic information, such as:

Size of finished, printed photo: This will help the photographer decide which film and equipment to use.

Page layout: This gives the photographer a better sense of the function of the photographs.

Props: Indicate necessary and optional accessories to the products.

Style: If you have a "look" in mind for the appearance of the photograph, this is where you should explain and describe it as clearly as you can.

If you are designing a fashion spot, you will want to include the specifics about the models, location details, and the color and lighting treatment. Color and light can be so variable in photographs that it is wise to give the photographers a few examples of photos that are close in style or treatment to what you are after. This way, the photographer can better understand what you are after.

Photographers, like illustrators, develop personal styles with which they come highly skilled. It can be a waste of time, talent and money to use the wrong photographer for the wrong job. A skillful table top and product photographer might not be the best choice for an architectural assignment or a fashion shot. An architectural photographer might not be the best one to shoot a board of directors photo for an annual report. A portfolio review should help you decide if a photographer you are considering would do the best job for you.

Working with Existing Photographs

In some situations you will have to work with existing photographs. Sometimes a client will have a photo

The comp of this catalogue came very close to duplicating the composition of the final printed piece. The main drawing was done with fine tip felt marker. The darker areas were done on the reverse of tissue paper, which was then spray glued and mounted to the cover stock.

A reduced photocopy of the photograph was mounted to the comp to demonstrate how the final layout will appear. Although the line values and darks in the photographs are much stronger than in the final piece, some designers purposely exaggerate the contrast of the comp, so that it doesn't look soft and weak.

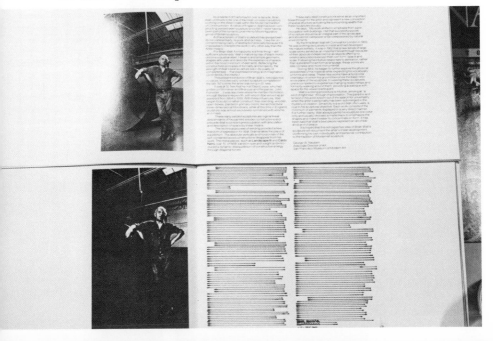

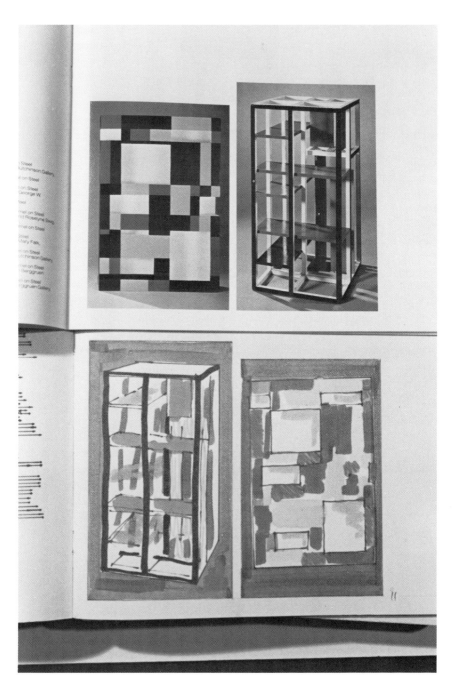

The photographs in this catalogue were also indicated on the comp with felt marker on tissue paper.

library of images that his company uses for training, promo-
tion, historic, or even personal reasons. Perhaps your subject is journalistic or illustrates an event that has already
occurred. Perhaps the budget won't allow for new photographs to be taken. Maybe the subject or theme of the design project is too broad for one photographer to capture.
This could require using existing photographs from stock
photo agencies. How do you incorporate existing photographs into a rough, comp or mock-up?

Sketching: The most obvious way to translate the image is
to sketch it to scale onto the comp or rough. You can do this
freehand, or with the aid of a Lucygraph or Artograph machine. As with illustration roughs and comps, use the same
degree of finish to the sketch as you would for the rest of
the details like headlines and type. For example, if you have
carefully rendered each headline character and dutifully
ruled each text line, your sketch of the photo should be rendered to similar detail, with basic composition and detail
lines in place, and the color carefully chosen. However, if
your rough is very loose and somewhat vague, your drawing can be as well. The tighter the comp, the tighter the
image should be. If you decide that a sketch is inadequate
to represent the photograph, you may choose to reproduce
the photograph to scale for the comp. There are several
ways to do this. If your photograph is black and white,
there are two options: make a xerographic copy from a variable sizing copier or have a scaled enlarged print made. The
later process offers more quality control, since you can specify contrast and paper type. The copier technique will usually provide you with an extremely high contrast image,
often with unsatisfactory results. Naturally, the enlarged
photo print method is more expensive, and time consuming, than the copier machine method.

Color photographs offer several reproduction alternatives. Color transparency film, be it 35mm slides, 2¼ ×
2¼", or 4" × 5" or 8" × 10", is popular with photographers

for many good reasons. Color transparencies are made with a variety of film types. Color separators find them easier to work with than prints or flat art, and lab processing for transparencies is substantially less expensive than enlarged color prints. Since the film that records the image in the camera is the film from which the color separator will work, it is a direct material process.

This comp of a cover for a catalogue is prepared with an "R" print of the cover photograph, and the title is a reverse photostat.

STEPHEN DE STAEBLER

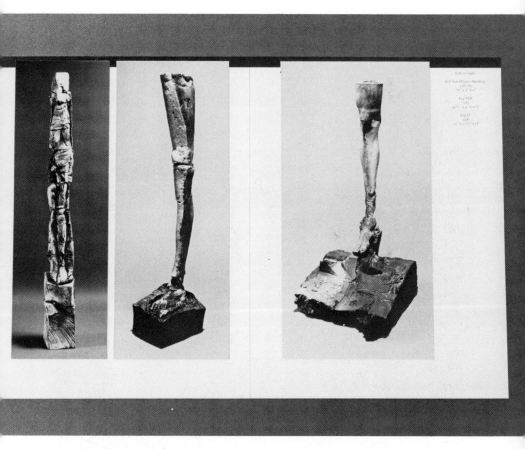

A typical spread from the previous catalogue consists of "R" prints and a photostat, mounted on matteboard.

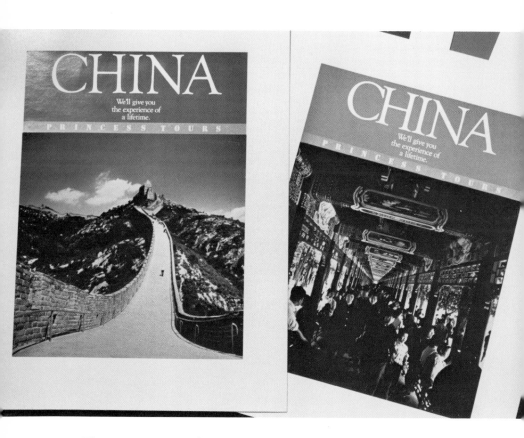

These two options for the cover of a catalogue were fully comped with photographs, custom rubdown transfers and colored paper, mounted flat on matteboard.

"C" and "R" Prints: A designer preparing a comp requiring a scaled reproduction of the image can have a "C" print or an "R" print made. The "C" print requires an internegative—an additional production step that makes a regular enlargement print negative from the transparency. That internegative can then be printed onto color enlargement print paper for the finished product. You could avoid that internegative step by having an "R" print made from the transparency. An "R" print is enlarged directly from the original film. The disadvantage of the "R" print is that some color and detail qualities are often lost and value contrast is increased. Though the quality of "R" prints is increasing because of improved printing papers and techniques, "C" prints are usually better quality. If the photographer used print film instead of transparency film, you can have a color print negative to begin with, you can have a "C" print made without going through the step of making an internegative. A custom photo lab should be able to tell you what to expect from your original transparency.

Occasionally, color xerographic copies from slides are adequate for roughs and comps. Although the scale range is limited, some applications are successful with this technique. Test your job first before relying on this process.

A step or two more defined than the color xerographic process is a color stat technique. It is more expensive than xerography, but it has significant features like variable reduction and enlargement capabilities, higher quality, and remarkable speed. Price is slightly less than color photography prints. The color rendition is usually better in a color photo print than it is in a color stat, but it is especially handy when you don't have the time to use the photographic print method.

V
Color Comping Techniques

Approaches to color comps

Any of the traditional comping techniques work wonderfully—if you know how to use them. Colored pencils used on the proper surface, guided by an experienced hand can produce as tight a comp as color pastels, inks, gouache, or felt pens. The trick is to know how to draw convincingly onto the proper surface.

Since this is not a book on illustration, we will not discuss rendering techniques with these materials. Instead, we will talk about some of the short cuts, tricks, or recent developments in graphic materials that rely less on an illustrator's ability than clever application and fast thinking. But before we proceed, a word of suggestion for designers who prefer to rely on the traditional materials. Though there is nothing wrong, of course, with an ability to draw, to handle paint, or to render well, clumsy application is obvious and can work against you. An example of this can be seen in much student work and student portfolios. The range of techniques most students are familiar with is impressive, but the results are frequently disappointing. How much better it would be for a typical student to spend more time developing one or two styles very well.

If a designer can draw well but has trouble with paint or ink or the looser media, then he should stick to pencils and felt pens, obviously. As mentioned throughout this book, a successful designer develops a presentation vocabulary that becomes more refined with experience. Keep in mind, however, it is the design itself that requires the most attention. The form that design takes in the presentation should become secondary. The presentation is a means of explanation only, not the end result.

Let's discuss some of these graphic materials that don't rely on rendering skill. There are many ways to apply color directly to the paper surface for comps and roughs. The experience and proficiency of the designer will determine the best method for each assignment.

Traditional Methods

The dry methods include colored pencils, chalk pastels, and oil pastels. These materials are more workable than the wet methods: the color can be pulled up or erased, and they lend themselves to blending and mixing. When properly used, they can produce very subtle or intense color effects. Colored pencils are good for tight detail work, lettering, and drawing. Pastels are great for large, flat areas. The dry methods can be used on lots of kinds of paper surfaces, from matboard to tissue paper.

The wet methods include pen and ink, brush and ink, and watercolor. The wet methods all affect the paper surface. Many papers are too thin to withstand the warping and shrinkage that wet methods produce. On illustration board, watercolor paper, or properly sized and stretched paper, the moisture isn't as much of a problem. Since drawing surface is so important, let's investigate some papers and their qualities.

Tracing Paper

Of all the materials and tools used by the graphic designer, tracing paper is certainly one of the most versatile. It is often the first surface on which a designer will develop an idea, and it is often used for the final mock up. It is available in a wide selection of weights, sizes, and quality grades, from inexpensive rolls to large sheets of fine tracing vellum, sturdy and white, just translucent enough to be useful for tracing, but hard enough to be satisfactorily used with technical pens.

At the start of a design job, a designer might use a basic form or type style, and then begin to draw variations and elaborations of that idea. As the ideas form, develop, evolve, and reconstruct, the designer can keep up with this process by quickly tracing the original form, with drawn variation.

With the result of as many possible solutions to the design, they can be taped to the wall, compared, reviewed, and rejected or selected. The similarity in size and style will allow for an equal basis on which to make a selection.

The next stage in the design will be to make refinements, and here, too, tracing paper is helpful to the process of designing the major and the subtle details. The materials you use are relevant to the effects you will achieve. Your design is influenced by your drawing tools. Fine line drawings will require a crow quill or technical pen. Some tracing papers are soft and will cause solvent-based inks to bleed.

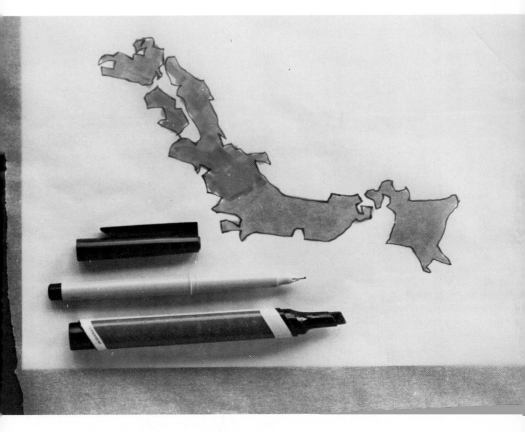

Notice the two different textures that the felt marker creates. The top of the illustration shows the felt marker placed on the back of the tissue. The lower portion shows the ink on the surface of the tissue.

Some water-based felt tip pens don't absorb into the paper and smear very easily. Sometimes color pencils are the best way to indicate color on tracing tissue, sometimes, felt pen inks are the best solution.

On this presentation board, the designer has prepared a series of logo design options for the client. They are tightly rendered and unambiguous.

Designers who use tracing paper develop their own tricks with the different grades they use. Some designers use the front of the paper for the line work, outlining the general illustration or photographic compositions, text type, or headline type in black, and then use the back of the paper to lay down felt marker color. This is especially effective on a medium to light weight paper that is very transparent. More opaque paper lightens the color too much. The lighter papers curl easily, though, and can be sprayed with an aerosol adhesive so that they can be mounted onto the paper of the comp.

Good quality tracing vellums are heavy enough so that they may not need to be mounted, but color application will require careful thought because of the paper's opaque nature.

The ultimate success of any color comp is its effectiveness to portray the end printed result. While a designer may, indeed, be able to handle pen, ink, felt marker, tempera, pastels, or color pencils, the effect has to approximate the finished printed piece. That result is often easier to achieve with the following techniques. Most of these are newer processes.

Indirect Processes

When a designer produces a design on a piece of paper, he is working directly. When a designer is using rubdown lettering, zip films, cut-out plastic textures, tapes for borders, colored paper, or color comping materials, he is working with indirect processes.

The chief advantage of these techniques is their mechanical, very tight quality that closely resembles the look of the finished printed piece. The human hand, no matter how steady, has a difficult time duplicating those results. Let's take these materials in turn, and examine their qualities for preparing effective color comps.

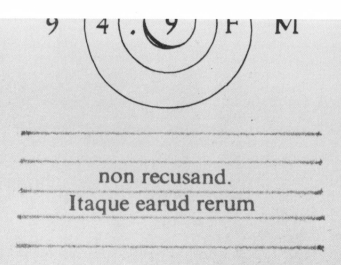

non recusand.
Itaque earud rerum

This detail shows custom-made rubdown transfers. Since this design is so delicate, it would be difficult, if not impossible, to properly indicate it in any other way. The design is a strong color on a grey paper. The rule below the main logo is a felt tip pen line. The second figure shows Greeking in a third color. The finish and approximate color—extra production steps—make the design much more convincing to the client at the presentation stage of the design process.

The final design of the logo was converted to rubdown transfer type. Greeking was photocopied onto colored paper before the logotype was applied.

Rubdown Type

In Chapter II we discussed ways to illustrate type in roughs, comps and mock-ups. The same techniques work for color, but we can add one: the color transfer type.

Color transfer type is available by three methods. The first is to buy color rubdown type. The primary limitations of this approach is that only a few typefaces, in a few sizes, are available in a few basic colors. It would be a simple matter to find 48 point Helvetica in primary red or navy blue, for example. However, if you need 48 point Palatino italic in a warm grey, you won't find it in the transfer lettering catalogues.

Although, you can get Palatino Italic in white. You could transfer the type onto your comp, and then color each of the white letters grey with a felt pen.

While that might be acceptable for 48 point type, 12 point type would be too difficult. Another more refined method is to have rubdown type custom made to the color you need. This is becoming more popular with designers who need tight and accurate color comps to present to their clients. This technique involves having a typesetter set all of the type you want made into rubdowns, in the sizes and styles you will need for the final comp. You simply locate an outlet for custom rubdowns. Some photostat houses and typesetting companies are offering this service now. They use the same color matching system as printers, which makes the process highly accurate, simple, and effective. There is an expense for this method, of course, and you should investigate this cost so that you aren't surprised. The less you order and the fewer the colors, the less the expense will be.

Many designers have grown so accustomed to using custom rubdowns to produce tight type, logotypes, logo designs, and spot illustrations that they automatically include those expenses into their initial bids. Many firms use these custom rubdowns. The professional, tight, and clean look of these rubdowns on a comp can cut out the uncertainty and ambiguity of the design for a client. In other words, the expense is easily justified.

This comp was prepared with gummed, coated color paper cut into strips. The type was drawn with ink and felt marker.

Plastic color films and solid color paper

One of the hardest textures to duplicate with felt markers, pencil, watercolor, inks and paints is a smooth even layer of color. That is what colored films and paper do best.

Sold in sheets, these plastic films come in many colors; they are matched to printing inks, and they have an adhesive side. They are transparent, so that you can see outlines, type, or texture through the color.

Typically, a designer will cut out a piece slightly larger than the area of the final color. With an x-acto knife, the outline of the color is cut and the excess film is removed. The remaining color is carefully burnished, from the center out, to remove trapped air pockets from under the film. Since the film is transparent, these air pockets will show up unless they are removed. Pricking them with a sharp tool and pressing the bubble of air out will work better than trying to remove the film and reapplying it, especially if the air pocket is trapped in the middle of a large area.

Combining layers of different colors will create secondary colors that approximate the effect of stacking one ink on another, but the effect is *only approximate*.

As with any materials, practice with these films on a piece of scrap paper before committing them to final art. Putting these adhesive films down on carefully drawn art and then deciding that the effect isn't right could destroy the base art if you have to remove the plastic color.

Colored Papers

Solids in design and advertising projects are important. The smoother and more even the color, the more convincing they appear. Pantone paper is available in two forms: a coated adhesive solid color paper and uncoated solid color paper. The selection is greater in the latter, but the effect of the color is substantially subdued. These papers can be cut and applied in pieces, or used as a base on which to be drawn or pasted.

A new product is graduated color paper. Several commonly used colors are available, ranging from solid tint to a lighter value of the same color. These papers are available in a variety of surfaces.

Textured films

Similar in application and effectiveness, textured films are black-and-white line representations of symbols, architectural materials, herringbone patterns, pebble and sand motifs, wood grain, dots, lines, squares, grids, circles, triangles, wavy lines, splashes, and any number of other graphic symbols and devices. These can be used with color films for combined effects.

Color xerox

Color xerox copies are appropriate for some applications, but because of the loss of color quality and accuracy, designers are frequently better off relying on photo prints ("C" prints and "R" prints) or color photo stats.

Imaginatively applied, however, color xerox offers some unusual possibilities. With the rougher color rendition and color shift, a variety of expressive results are possible. Some graphic illustrators working in collage styles have found the results especially effective.

Color xerox machines offer a wide range of effects. They can print on clear film, enlarge slides, make iron-on decals, and create color type from black and white originals. Speed, though, is its chief advantage.

The expense of color xerox copying can add up quickly. Since each copy costs, and since the copier might require some experimentation to get the effects you are looking for, you might be in for a more expensive effect than you expected.

Pinwheel, Chromatech and "polished comp" techniques

In the past few years a number of services and products have gained widespread popularity that help designers virtually duplicate a finished printed color piece. These techniques require no printing and they allow color variations at prices substantially less than on-press experimentation. Their only drawback is that the cost of these techniques is just high enough that you may get resistance from your client about using them. For many projects, though, the extra persuasion it may take on your part is worth it.

The Pinwheel system is a nationally marketed technique available through a network of typography and photostat houses. Using this method of color comping, you prepare camera ready artwork as you would for a printer, to size. Then, on a tissue, you call out the pins colors you want to use on the final printed piece. You also furnish some sheets of the paper on which the final job will be printed. The technician will shoot film from the artwork, mix the colors, and then print the piece onto the furnished stock, registering the colors into place. As with printing you will be charged by the size of the image, the complexity of the filmwork, and the number of colors printed.

You may specify color a number of ways at this stage, or you can order one color combination and modify the colors when you see what it looks like. Since any pins color is available in this system, and since the actual paper stock is being used, you are getting as accurate a comp as you can get without going to press.

This technique is best for line art. Screens and halftones can be reproduced, but with less success. Color photographs cannot be reproduced in this method as successfully as with a "C" or "R" print, so you will probably want to duplicate the line art and solids with the Pinwheel method, and then mount photographs into position as a final step.

Chromateck

A related product with wide application potential is custom rubdown chromateck. Basically, this technique works just like rubdown type, except that you provide the type, textures, drawings, symbols, illustrations, or logos that you want in rubdown form. You can also select the pins color you want to use. As with any rubdown material, you can apply it to the actual stock that will be used on the job.

This process also requires camera ready line art or type, but since you determine the spacing and placement, you can gauge many images onto a single sheet. Some designers will cram as much as they possibly can onto a sheet. (8" × 10" and 5" × 8" are common sizes).

For this technique you are billed by the number of sheets you order, the size of each sheet, and the number of colors you order.

VI
Mock-Up Techniques

In the introduction, we defined mock-up as a facsimile of a printed or constructed design product. A three-dimensional model or assembled, one-of-a-kind representation. Experienced designers can tell when a client is "getting it"—comprehending the design concept. Many designers insure that their clients "get it" by preparing mock-up comps. The form the mock-ups take is as varied as the products they represent.

Few clients can resist the appeal of a mock-up. Architects know how a scale model of a building can excite a boardroom of normally somber executives. There is something universally fascinating about seeing a project in its evolutionary stage, and for a designer, this is in the mock-up.

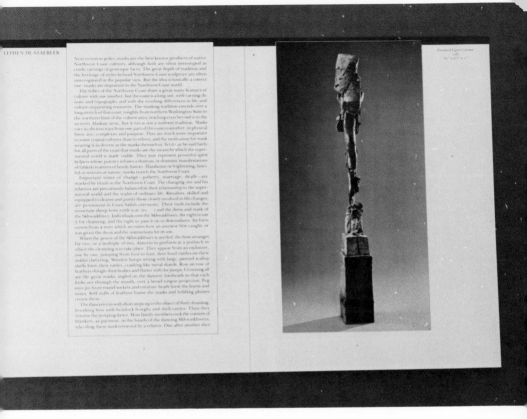

Type design, rules, placement of folio, captions, and page layout are all clearly illustrated in this comp.

Mock-up of Books, Catalogues, and Annual Reports

Most major paper distributing companies have sample departments. They understand the importance of the mock-up to sell printing jobs to the clients of designers. This can be a great resource for the designer.

Once you have designed the job, determined the paper, cover stock, size, and binding method, you can have a sample department at the paper company prepare a mock-up to your specifications that will give you the basic form of the final product.

In this basic, unprinted form, the mock-up will have a weight and presence to it. The client will be able to pick it up, to feel the cover, check the weight and texture of the paper, and will get an immediate impression. This is important to the success of many presentations. It is closer to reality at this stage than any two-dimensional presentation board.

The presentation boards, though, are important for showing the subtleties of the design elements. It is here that you can explain column widths, use of photographs, typographic style and function, and use of color. All of these qualities are easier to explain to a client when they are flat and mounted, because you can set the board up and get the client a little further away. This helps him to see the general design, instead of specific details, and allows you to point them out. Presentation boards are essential for presentations to more than one viewer.

Some designers choose to prepare a blank mock-up to present first. "This is how large and how many pages your report will be," a designer might explain. This sets the finished product in the client's mind. Next, the designer will display the presentation board, carefully explaining the details. Finally, to set the impression firmly in the client's mind, the designer will hand the client a comp mock-up like the blank mock-up, except with the cover, and first pages (or even all of the pages) complete. This mock-up should have examples of all of the stylistic points you made from the presentation boards.

At this stage, you ask for the client's approval; if not for all of the details, at least the design concept and direction.

Identity Programs

Depending upon the size of the company and the complexity of their needs, identity program presentations can range from simple, friendly, informal meetings to elaborately staged extravaganzas that would startle a Las Vegas stage director. Saul Bass is legendary in the design profession for sparing no expense, or showman technique, in presenting an idea to a client with extremely high visability.

Ultimately, however, you face two issues: having a good design solution, and selling that design to the client. The designer is responsible for the first point, and the second requires careful preparation.

This comp of a letterhead was prepared with custom rubdowns of the type and logo. The typewritten section is intended to duplicate a common letter as it appears on the new letterhead design.

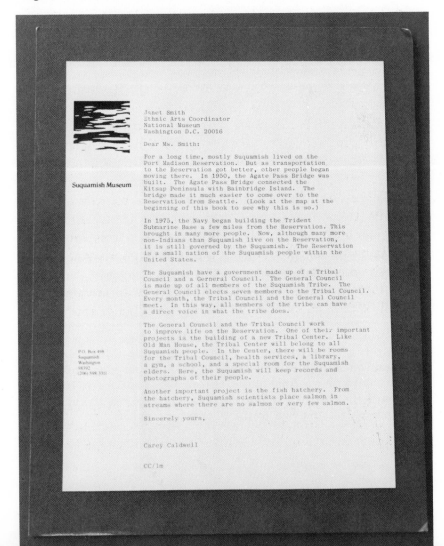

The designers anticipated that this logo would be used in a variety of printed applications, so they needed to show the client how three special effects might look. In the first application, color printing on colored paper, the designer duplicated this effect by cutting the logo out of color overlay film, and applying it to colored paper. The second figure shows how the logo might appear as a blind embossed design on metallic paper. The logo was cut out of the same paper as the base and glued onto the background. In the final figure, the logo is illustrated as it might appear foil stamped on colored paper. The logo here is cut out of foil paper and attached to the background paper.

These parts of the identity program were also prepared with rub-down transfer, in two colors.

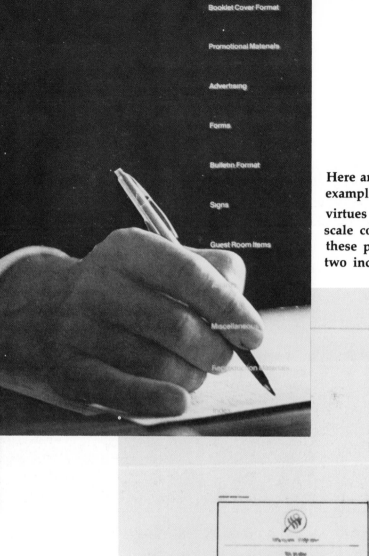

Here are some more examples illustrating the virtues of reduced scale comps. Each of these pages is only two inches tall.

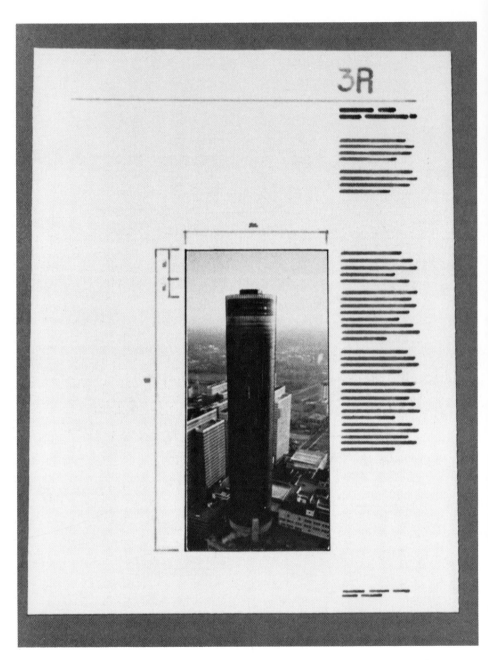

Photographs have been pulled from stock files, and the type is custom made rubdown transfer. The individual pages have been

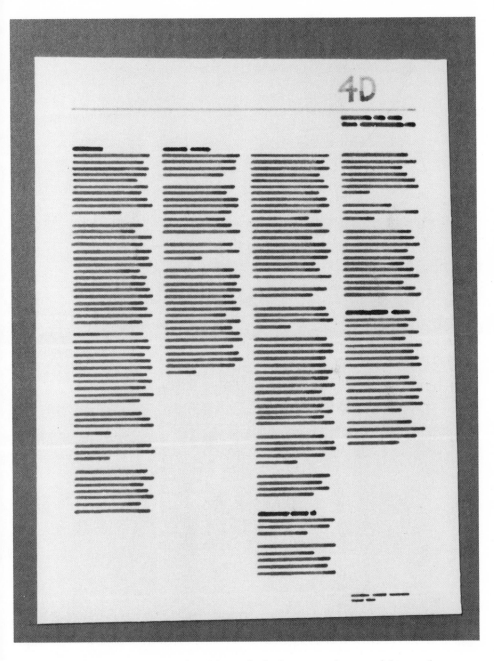

carefully represented with technical pen rules or felt marker lines in the appropriate colors.

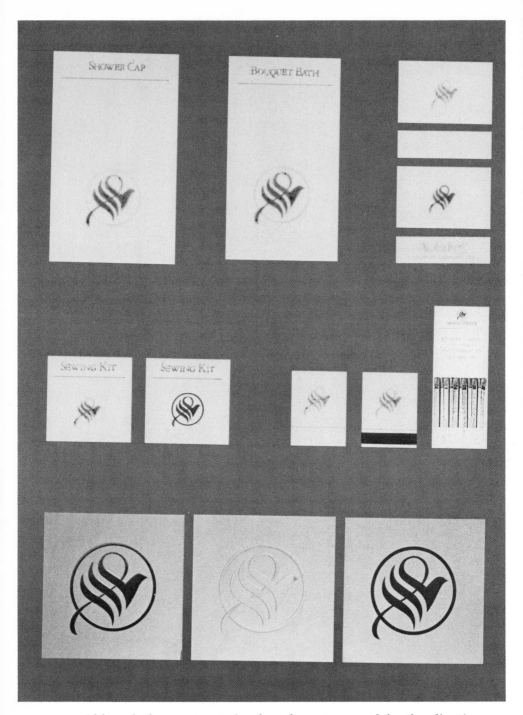

Although these presentation boards are prepared for the client's benefit, they certainly help the designer to maintain a clear overview of the various applications of a logo design. These products

are represented on the presentation board to scale, in colors approximating the final printed piece.

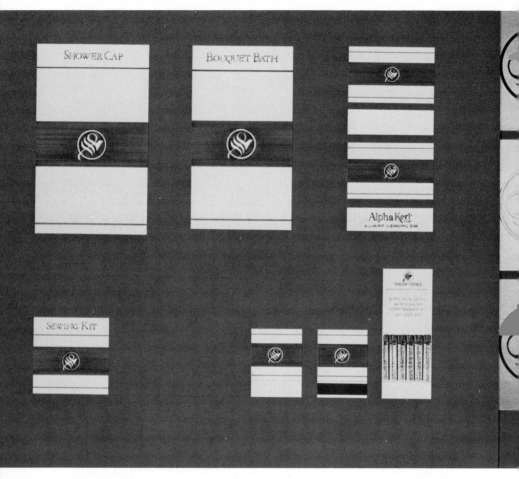

Designers and clients often need to see design alternatives before proceeding with the selected design. They should all be prepared to the same degree of finish for an accurate comparison.

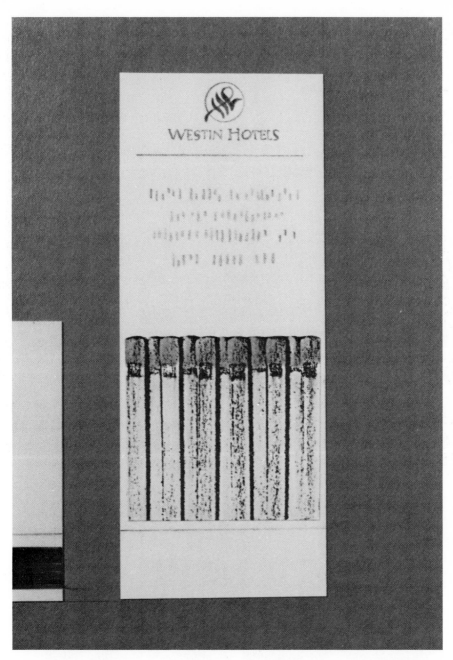

This mock-up of a matchbook was prepared by photocopying matches from a real matchbook and coloring them in with felt marker.

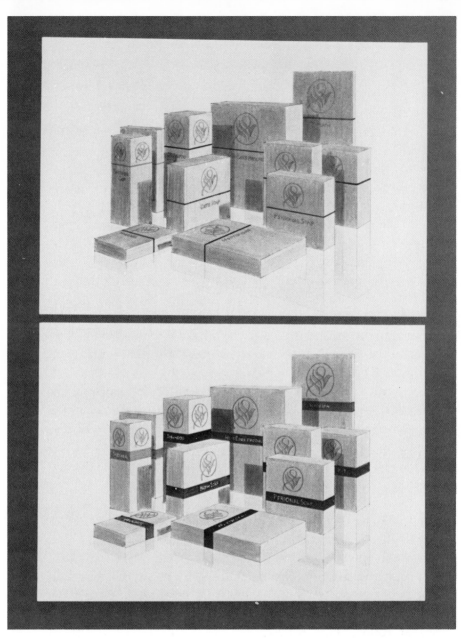

Package design options can be simply and effectively presented by drawing, instead of constructing them three-dimensionally. Here, the same drawing was duplicated and then inked in many different ways. For additional variations, the guidelines of the drawing could be indicated very faintly on a master drawing, which, in turn, could be photocopied on white or colored paper. The designer used felt markers to indicate color.

Logos

Most identity programs have a logo or logotype, or some central element around which everything else is based. This element can be drawn, enlarged photographically, and mounted on a presentation board. The logo is simple to present.

Logos, however, are not often used out of context. They exist in ads, letterheads, business cards, signage, on the sides of vehicles, as lighted signs on top of tall buildings, engraved cufflinks, as discreet patterns on silk scarves, and as stenciled lables on the sides of rough wooden crates. A successful logo works on any application where it will be required. In preparing a presentation for an identity program, decide how your design will be used initially, and how it might be used eventually.

Your list will include business stationery, since that is an almost universal requirement for businesses. Letterheads, envelopes, business cards, shipping labels, invoices, purchase orders, bid sheets, internal memo sheets, statements, billing envelopes, postcards. Even that list can go on and on. The first three items are the most common for even the smallest business, so let's start there.

The letterhead is a good piece of business stationery with which to start. It is also a reasonable size so that you can easily prepare a mock-up to actual size with minimum expense and trouble. The letterhead should be presented on the paper stock it will be printed on, samples of which can be obtained from paper distributors or printers. (An additional good reason for locating the actual paper sample is that you can simultaneously check on the availability of that stock. A designer often encounters frustration when he specifies a certain paper from a distributor's sample book, only to discover that there is a huge minimum order requirement, or that a particular tone, color, or texture has been discontinued. Thwarting these possible frustrations before the presentation makes your work later much simpler.

A multiple letterhead presentation is an effective way to show off the qualities of your design. After you have explained the logo, talk about the importance of a good-looking letter. Explain how you arrived at your design solution, and then unveil the letterhead, mounted on a presentation board. Talk about the elements of the letterhead. Next, hand the client a sample sheet of the paper, either blank or with the design comped on it. Then, on another presentation board, show the letterhead with a letter typed on it, with date, address, greeting, letter body, paragraph spacing or indentation, closing salutation, and folds just as you would have them. Explain the rationale for these elements. Finally, show a sheet of the stationery, xerox-copied to show how well the type and logo can be reproduced on a typical copier.

With these features properly explained, pull out the envelope comp. It should be addressed as a typical business letter might be, and stamped, since these are constants on any business letters.

The business card is the next stage. Business card stock is an important consideration for most clients. They invariably ask what weight it will be printed on. Make sure you have an actual sample of the stock you have in mind. The client will wonder if it is heavy enough. It is a good idea to have several examples of other business cards on hand to show comparative thicknesses of stock. (The larger and more prestigious the company you use as an example, the more persuasive your argument will be.)

After you have presented the logo alone, the letterhead, the envelope, and the business card, you should have a good idea of how the design is being received. Some of the most successful designers have found that the more applications they can devise for the logo for the presentation, the more likely the client is to accept the design—assuming, of course, that the design is a successful solution to the client's problems. Why this reaction? It probably allows the logo design to exist in real life surroundings: it looks less abstract when it is stenciled on the side of a coffee mug, than it does stark, big, and daring on a presentation board. Here we have another situation where the presentation board is essential to help give the client a good look at a design. The three-dimensional form then, helps the client to "get it."

From this point, showing the logo in context requires thought and design sensitivity, but if the client generally likes and approves of the logo, specific applications can be presented with more focus on the item than on the logo itself. You've already addressed the design problem on an abstract level.

Unusual approaches to identity application need to be presented with special care: it is easy to scare an otherwise convinced client by an idea that looks too aggressive or ahead of its time. Once a client bolts, it's hard to lure him back without substantial compromise to your design.

Say, for example, you want to have a skywriter emblazen the new logo over a major metropolitan area on the clearest, sunniest summer day. It might be just the way to introduce the identity to hundreds of thousands of people. You have, however, just convinced him, finally, that the stock of the business card *is* heavy enough. Now is not the time to bring up the skywriting idea. Save that for when the compliments for the handsome new stationery come pouring in, and then try your luck and persuasive skill.

Full-blown identity programs can take months to prepare, but the presentation process is much less nerve racking, since the basic design and direction is approved. Your goal at this point is to fill in the gaps, and then show to your client the results of your efforts, which should be within the bounds of his initial approval.

Video Story Boards

A conceptual television presentation confronts the designer and client with additional problems. First, since the primary feature of video is movement and constant change, and since production expenses for presentation usually limit the designer to static representation, this establishes a major hurdle to the client's (and even the designer's) previsualization of the end result. If we don't have budgets to create enactments or movement models, we are left with a cartoon-type sequence of the episode. If we view this situation as a good newspaper cartoonist approaches his own situation, we can learn a few techniques and pointers.

It is easy for us to imagine cartoon characters as having real lives. In fact, they have lives only in still images. They will never actually be put into motion. Instead, movement is suggested by an arsenal of graphic devices, from the simple transitory expression on the characters' faces, to ZAPS, POWS, and BOOMS that surround the characters in tightly-cropped frames.

The traditional approach to staging a commercial is to script the dialogue and to imagine the action and sequence. Then, the presentation sequence board freezes images along the course of the narrative. Naturally, important transitions are captured, and the impression one has looking at the final board is of stop action.

A skilled presentor can, in the telling of the narrative, bring these characters or situations alive for the client, and that is the advantage you have over the newspaper cartoonist: you have both the image and the spoken characterization to get your message to the client.

This process assumes that you have a good script that addresses the client's needs. With that, you need a good set of story board illustrations that are refined enough to be convincing, but vague enough to allow you the freedom of selecting details at a later stage.

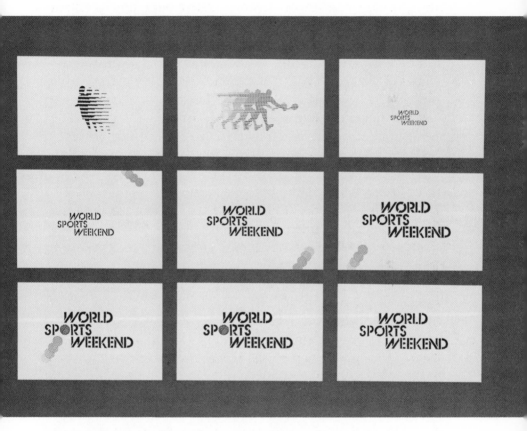

This sequential presentation board shows how video animation
will work for opening credits to a television show.

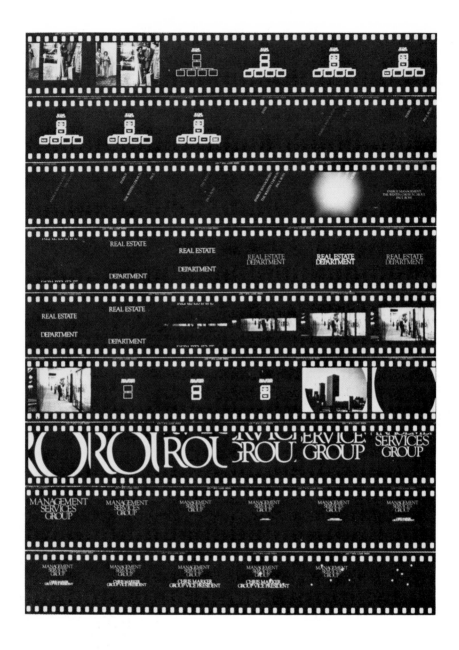

A complex slide presentation is explained in these film strips. It is much easier to see the entire show at a glance using this method than it is to try to remember all of the images in sequence.

One stagey but effective technique to heighten the sensation of watching an actual video progression is to cover the images with paper. During the course of the narration, remove each sheet one by one. This allows the client some of the sensation of seeing the commercial for the first time.

Another way to present sequential visuals for video is to shoot slides of the artwork and project it in a dark room. This, naturally, allows each image more impact, and the sequencing of the slides carries the story line along. The chief disadvantage is that the original drawings need to be tightly rendered to survive such enlargement.

Signage Mock-Ups

Signage communicates to the reader. It is environmental, and works only in its proper setting. A door sign does little good anywhere except on the proper door. This means that when you design signage, its setting becomes as important as the signage itself. Designers usually find it important to represent the setting and scale of the signage. This can be done in a variety of ways.

Quick sketches are the simplest approach. A good sketch can successfully communicate scale, location, and the function of the signage in general terms. The quality of the quick sketches will determine how impressive the presentation will be. Tighter drawings will convey more authority, however.

Models of signage can be enticingly convincing. Small scale cardboard cutouts, with type, color, and construction details made a three-dimensional appeal to most clients, just as architectural models and interior miniatures appeal to most children and adults.

Signage problems can be visualized in scale models and drawings. This designer sketched his design solutions first, then constructed models. The successful cardboard models were then photographed from different angles. Traced drawings were made from the photographs, with color options indicated on the drawings. The type design, on the model before it was photographed, made it very much easier to render from the photographs.

The three-dimensional model should be accompanied by an indication of scale, if it's not immediately apparent. Typically, this might be a cardboard silhouette or profile of an individual or group.

The three-dimensional model should be accompanied representation of its setting, depending upon the client's ability to visualize the setting. Material models are helpful for conveying an impression of the effect of the material details, especially when the elements are unusual, rich, or selected in unusual juxtaposition. These models allow designers to test the workability of materials before the job is approved and specified. These models are most impressive when they are presented, in whole or in part, at actual scale.

Another aspect of a blueline that can be especially deceiving is half-tone reproduction. Bluelines can indicate whether the halftone negative is clean and free of dust or dirt, but you can't really tell how the halftone will look once it is printed. A black and white photo contact print, a black color key made from the printer's negative, or a press proof are the only ways to check the quality of a halftone, if its reproduction quality is in doubt.

With all design jobs, the client should be given the blueline to check for accuracy and details, and they should sign their approval for that blueline. This approval protects the designer if a mistake is discovered on the final printed piece.

Cromalins

Designers and clients need to see how well the color photographs are going to reproduce before the job goes to stripping. Printers also need to know what colors they are expected to match. When a transparency or color print is separated into four process colors, proofs can be made from the film from that process. One method is to make a Cromalin, which is a film and paper sandwich with color powders duplicating the effects of color ink. The result is one copy of the color transparency, the size it will be in print. Viewed under 5000°K lights, the color should come close to the color of the original transparency or color print from which the separation is made.

The Cromalin is usually a little greyer and duller than it will appear in print, since you are seeing the color through four layers of clear plastic, which dull the white of the base paper. If you notice distinct color shifts, you should request that the separations be corrected to compensate. You may want to order a corrected Cromalin to check the color correction.

Since the light source is crucial to the way we perceive color, it is important that you and your client view the Cromalin under proper light. Cromalins in daylight will not give you an accurate impression of the color of the separation.

Another proof method is the Color Key. This process involves four layers of loose plastic over a sheet of paper, registered, and taped into place. Each layer of film carries one of the process colors: yellow, magenta, cyan, and black. The composite duplicates the four process colors printed on paper. A similar greying happens with this process. In fact, the grey is even darker than it is on the Cromalin because the plastic layers are thicker than they are on the Cromalin.

Both techniques can be used on built or stacked screen colors. Let's say that you have specified a block of color made with 10% black, 10% cyan, 80% magenta, and 90% yellow, the Cromalin or the Color Key will be able to approximate that mixture before the job goes to press.

Cromalins are not appropriate for previsualizing non-process colors. Color Keys are available in some of the more popular color printing inks, though. A designer might want to use the two techniques together: the Cromalin for the process color parts of the design, and a Color Key overlay for the PMS color sections. Check with your color separator for his advice.

Press Proofs

There is only one way to get an absolutely secure comp, and that is to go to the press proof stage. Though you may have completed all of the previous stages, some very critical jobs require that they be run on a press, on the actual paper that will be used, under the same conditions that the final job will be subjected, to make certain that the details of the job are correct. This is an expensive step, and usually cannot be justified to most clients, but on unusually large or important projects, the extra expense is a necessary one for many clients and designers.

Some press proof checks are supervised by the designer and client at the printing company. Sometimes, the press checks are sent to the designer to review, and then are returned with corrections marked on them for the printer.

As with any of these techniques, if you see a problem or have a question about the final result, investigate your concerns at that time. The closer to final press the mistake is discovered, the more expensive the change will be to make, but it will never be more expensive to make the change than it will be to reprint the entire job.

VII
Secure Comps

Bluelines, Cromalins, and Press Proofs

At the final stages of a design job, there are several points at which details and results of a job can be previewed. These techniques are checks on the aspects of the job that are more difficult to previsualize using comp techniques.

Bluelines

After your design job is sent to a printer, film negatives are shot of the artwork. These negatives are stripped together in the way they will be used to make the press plates. These negatives need to be exact and correct for the plates and printing to be correct.

From these negatives, a printer can make contact prints on blueline paper. Once trimmed and collated, this becomes an accurate representation of what the press plates will be able to produce. At this stage the designer catches last minute errors. Making changes after the blueline is made involves some expense, but not nearly as much as reprinting an incorrect job.

The three stages from comp to printed piece are illustrated in this photograph. The piece on the left is the comp. The center sheet is the blueline, and the piece on the right is the finished piece.

The most secure kind of proof is the press proof. In this example, the book is divided up into signatures; pages are glued together as they will appear in the bound book. Color quality is examined and adjusted. Dirt on the photographs and broken type are carefully corrected. This step is a luxury for many clients, but it is a necessity for others.

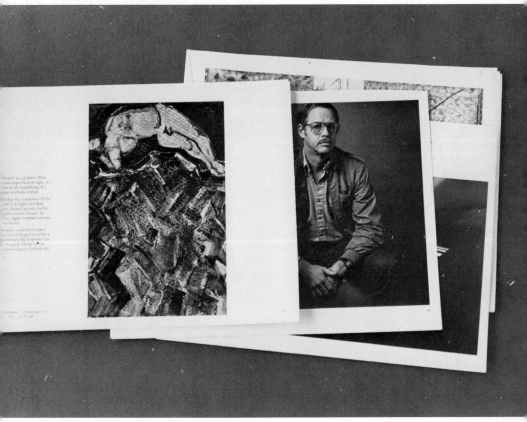

An annoying feature of the blueline is that the blue-line paper is yellow and when exposed to intense light, the type and printing parts of the design turn a light blue. Clients often have difficulty seeing the final design clearly because they are distracted by the pale blue and yellow. For both the designer and the client, it is very important to inspect the blueline carefully for misspellings, broken type, paste-up lines, flopped or misplaced photographs, missing page numbers, dirt in the halftones, crooked type, and inaccurate information.

Bluelines are deceiving though. For some perceptual reason, it is harder to catch mistakes on a blueline. Perhaps it is difficult to take the pale blue type as seriously as when it is in black and white. It is important, though, to concentrate on the type and details because it may be the last you see of the job before it goes to press.

Conclusion

As helpful as comps, roughs, and mock-ups may be to you and your client, you still have to sell the idea. For some designers that is more difficult than arriving at a design solution and comping it up. Here are some general suggestions that may be helpful to you.

1. If you have doubts about your verbal ability to sell your design, tight comps and mock-ups will be more helpful to you than roughs. Loose sketches require more verbal dexterity on the designer's part since you will, in effect, be completing the design in the client's mind by explaining your intention.

2. If you can think fast on your feet, you may purposely want a very rough mock-up to present to the client. (One well-known designer frequently makes her presentation to established clients on the backs of cocktail napkins over drinks. She has, of course, a proven record and firmly established trust with her clients. Still, she thinks that the informality of the presentation works to her advantage).

3. Don't get caught in the trap of preparing a comp that is simple to mock-up but extremely difficult to produce. A quick stroke of a felt pen might give you a wonderful effect on the comp, but you may be adding hundreds of dollars in extra color separations or passes through the press. Only comp up what the ultimate budget will allow, or you will set your client up for disappointment.

4. Make sure that the final printed piece looks better than the mock-up.

5. While making the presentation, write specific changes, alterations, or additions onto the mock-up clearly in the client's view so that both of you agree on the modifications. Some designers have the client sign the mock-up as assurance that the design has been approved. You will probably need the original comp to produce the final artwork. If you want to give the client the mock-up after the job is completed, that is your business, but if you have had to make many alterations to the final piece, you may find your client asking questions about those changes. The designer should keep the mock-up. If the client asks for it, xerox a copy for the client.

6. Most designers keep their mock-up after the job is printed. Clients often compare the mock-ups to the finished piece. This can cause unfortunate problems with clients who may notice subtle color shifts, type placement changes, or insignificant detail changes.

7. If you discover that you need to make significant changes to the design, notify your client immediately, explain the change, and get their approval.

8. Always try to be present during any presentation of your design work. No one can be counted on to

explain it better or more convincingly than the person who worked on it.

9. Always strive to polish your presentation technique.
10. Compromise wisely during the presentation.